Get set... GO!

Bang and Rattle

Sally Hewitt

Photography by Peter Millard

Contents

CP CHILDRENS PRESS®
CHICAGO

Introduction

Percussion instruments are played
by banging and rattling.
This makes the air around them vibrate.
This means the air moves back and forth
very, very fast, making the sound
that we hear.

Percussion instruments make
all kinds of different sounds.
You can bang the drum to the beat,
shake the maracas, rattle the cabaca,
slap the claves, click the castanets,
clash the cymbals, and strike the
chime bars and the xylophone.

Get ready to make some instruments
to bang and rattle.

448-9471

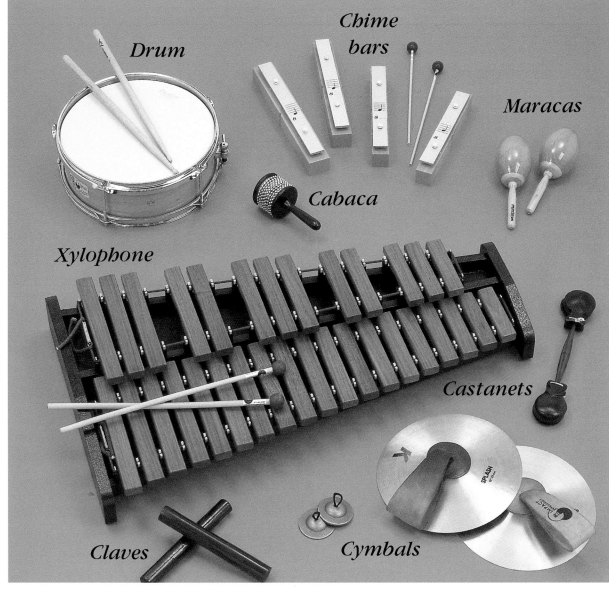

Drum

Chime bars

Maracas

Cabaca

Xylophone

Castanets

Claves

Cymbals

Shakers

Get ready

✔ Cans, boxes,
  plastic cups,
  all with lids

✔ Buttons, beads, pasta,
  rice, paper clips

. . . Get Set

Put a handful of pasta in a can.
Close the lid tightly.
Put some of the other things
in different containers and close the lids.

💨💨💨 *Go!*

Shake each of the containers.
Listen to the sounds they make.
Choose one shaker.
Shake it in time while you dance to music.

Rattles

Get ready

✔ Long piece of yarn
  or a shoelace
✔ Milk-bottle tops

✔ Buttons
✔ Macaroni
✔ Beads

. . . Get Set

Thread the objects onto
the yarn or shoelace.
Tie the ends together.

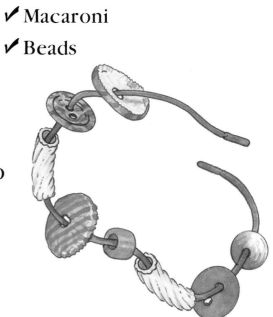

⚞⚞⚞ *Go!*

Shake your rattle.
Listen to the objects rattling together.
What kind of sounds do they make?

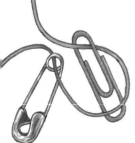

Janglers

Get ready

✔ String   ✔ Metal buttons   ✔ Paper clips

✔ Safety scissors   ✔ Metal curtain   ✔ Old keys

✔ Safety pins   rings
   (closed)

. . . Get Set

Cut a long piece of string.
Thread the metal objects
onto the string.
Tie the ends of the string together.

≈🌀≈🌀≈🌀 Go!

Shake your jangler.
Now shake your rattle (from page 6).
Listen to the different sounds
made by the rattle and the jangler.

Chimes

Get ready

✔ Coat hanger   ✔ Fork   ✔ Beater from
✔ Spoon   ✔ Pieces of string   electric mixer

. . . Get Set

Tie a piece of string onto the
spoon, the fork, and the beater.
Tie the other end of the string onto
the coat hanger.

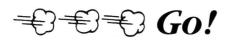 **Go!**

Hold up the coat hanger.
Tap the objects with a spoon.
Listen to them chime.
Hold the objects to stop them vibrating
and to deaden the sound.

Rollers

Get ready

✔ Cardboard tube ✔ Beads and marbles

✔ Safety scissors ✔ Rubber bands

✔ Construction paper

. . . Get Set

Cut two pieces of paper
larger than the ends of the tube.
Fasten one of the pieces of
paper over one end of the
tube with a rubber band.
Put the beads and marbles into the tube.
Cover the other end of the tube with paper and
fasten with a rubber band.

Go!

Roll the beads and marbles up and down.
Listen to the sound they make.

Raspers

Get ready

✔ 2 small boxes
✔ 2 pieces of sandpaper
✔ Pencil

✔ Glue
✔ Safety scissors

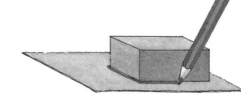

. . . Get Set

Place each box on the back of each piece of sandpaper. Draw around each box with a pencil.
Cut out the box shapes.
Glue the sandpaper, rough side up, onto the top of each box.
Let the boxes dry.

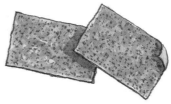

⸙⸙⸙ Go!

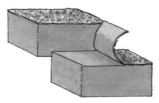

Rub the sandpaper sides together.
Listen to the rasping sound.

Scrapers

Get ready

- ✔ Comb
- ✔ Thin plastic lid
  (from a margarine tub)
- ✔ Small plastic cup
- ✔ Masking tape
- ✔ Safety scissors

. . . Get Set

Cut a strip from the plastic lid.
Fold it in half.
Fold back two small flaps at each end.
Tape the flaps to the bottom of the cup.

≈☁≈☁≈☁ *Go!*

Run your fingernail along
the teeth of the comb.
Listen to the rasping sound.
Now run the comb over the tab on the cup.
It makes a much louder sound.

Clappers

Get ready

✔ 2 lids   ✔ 2 spoons

✔ 2 plastic cups   ✔ 2 wooden blocks

✔ 2 pencils   ✔ 2 corks

. . . Get Set

Sort the objects into pairs.

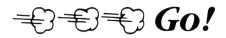

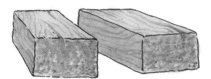

Go!

Clap and tap each pair of things together.
Listen to the sounds they make.
Can you make the sound of feet galloping,
tiptoeing, stamping, marching,
running, and dancing
with your clappers?

Drums and beaters

Get ready

- ✔ Boxes
- ✔ Cans
- ✔ Plastic containers
- ✔ Brushes
- ✔ Wooden spoons
- ✔ Metal spoons
- ✔ Pencils

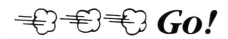

. . . Get Set

Group the drums and beaters by size.
Then group them by what they are made of.

Go!

Beat the drums with the spoons.
Listen to the sounds
made by big drums and little drums,
by plastic, wooden, and metal drums.
Different beaters can make
the same drum sound different.

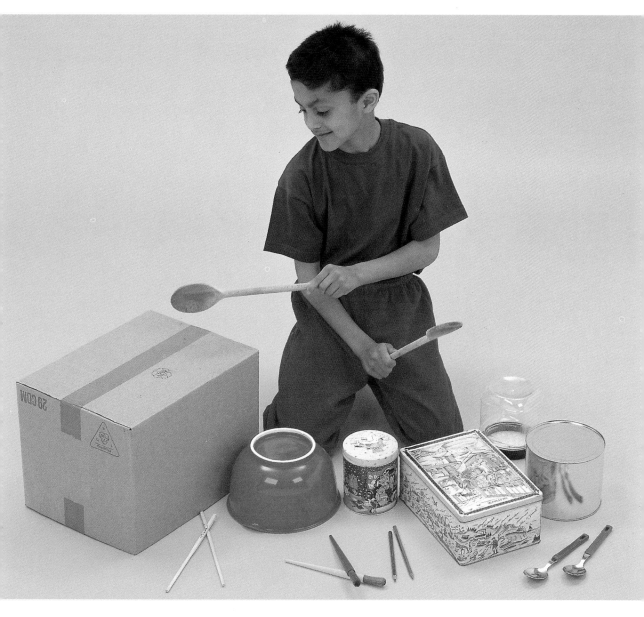

21

Make a drum

Get ready

- ✔ Cardboard box with one end open
- ✔ 2 wooden spoons
- ✔ String
- ✔ Plastic bag
- ✔ Safety scissors
- ✔ Masking tape

. . . Get Set

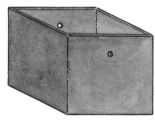

Ask an adult to make a hole in two opposite sides of the box. Cut a long piece of string. Thread the string through the holes in the box and knot the ends.

Stretch the plastic bag over the open end of the box. Tape it down tightly.
Put the string around your neck.

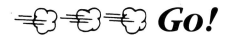 **Go!**

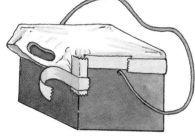

Now beat your drum with the wooden spoons.

Index

Acknowledgments: The author and publisher would like to thank the pupils of Kenmont Primary School, London, for their participation in the photographs of this book.

Editor: Pippa Pollard
Design: Ruth Levy
Cover design: Mike Davis
Artwork: Ruth Levy

Library of Congress Cataloging-in-Publication Data

Hewitt, Sally.
   Bang and rattle / by Sally Hewitt.
      p.   cm. — (Get set— go!)
   Includes index.
   ISBN 0-516-07987-5
      1. Percussion instruments—Juvenile literature. [1. Percussion instruments.] I. Title. II. Series.
ML1030.H49   1994
786.8′19—dc20   94-16948
                                                          CIP
1994 Childrens Press® Edition   AC
© 1993 Watts Books, London, New York, Sydney
All rights reserved. Printed in the United States of America.
Published simultaneously in Canada.
1 2 3 4 5 6 7 8 9 0 R 03 02 01 00 99 98 97 96 95 94

24